Searching for Rain in a Monsoon

Searching for Rain in a Monsoon

John Astin

∾

SANTA CRUZ, CALIFORNIA

Contents

Introduction

You do not acquire happiness. Your nature is happiness.

~ Ramana Maharshi

When Bill Moyers interviewed the renowned mythologist Joseph Campbell, he asked him what he thought human beings were searching for. Campbell answered that contrary to what most people believe, humans are not so much searching for a sense of meaning and purpose as they are a sense of aliveness. It's an intriguing notion—that what we're *really* searching for in this life is to feel that we are actually alive.

What's particularly striking about Campbell's statement, however, is that this aliveness we're supposedly searching for is something we already *are*. The very fact that we exist, and *know* we exist, is the one thing we can be certain of. The rest, we could say, is speculation. We may rightly question the reality of many things, but we can never with a straight face deny the reality of our own existence—because we would have to exist in the first place in order to do so!

No effort is required to bring this aliveness about. Existence is already here and fully present, awake in and as each one of us. The sense of aliveness Campbell speaks about isn't something we must somehow acquire through an exhaustive search or painstaking, effortful practice. It's already ours. Life needn't be sought so much as recognized to be what it is—present, inescapable and unavoidable. Everything is *already* dynamically alive, every thought, every sensation, every feeling, every sight, every sound, every taste, and every experience, completely, 100% present and vitally so. To search for a sense of aliveness when everything is already so vibrantly alive is like *searching for rain in a monsoon:* an unnecessary exercise. We are always and already drenched with life, soaked to the bone with this vitality that is everywhere and in everything.

Campbell tells a story that speaks very beautifully to this same theme of searching for something we already have. At a talk to physicians many years ago, he showed a series of slides depicting various religious symbols. When he got to the figure of Nataraja (the dancing Shiva of Hindu tradition), one of the attendees raised his hand and asked Campbell to speak about the meaning of the little dwarf-like person at the bottom of the statue, who appeared to be studying or gazing intently at something, Shiva's foot placed on top of him. This image is often explained as a symbol of Shiva's eradicating or stomping out our human ignorance and forgetfulness. But Campbell explained it this way: "The image of that little man captures our human predicament perfectly, searching in such earnest for the Divine when all along, we fail to realize that the living God is already here, dancing upon our very heads."

∾

In *Searching for Rain in a Monsoon,* you are invited through a series of meditative inquiries into an exploration of just this, the possibility that the very things we have been seeking after as humans—e.g., greater awareness, ease, clarity, love, and vitality, are already present as the *dynamic, unpredictable flow and movement of life itself.*

But by all means, please don't take my word for it. Check it out in your own direct experience and see if you don't (in the words of the poet, William Blake) discover worlds upon worlds in every grain of sand, heaven in the wildflowers, infinity in the palm of your hand, and eternity in every hour . . .

Meditations

The Miracle of Just This

We search for some other moment, a moment we imagine will be more fulfilling, more profound, more free, more meaningful . . . And yet, it is only when we demand something more from this moment, when we imagine what's here is somehow not quite enough, that we experience this heartache of incompleteness and then set about to find its resolution.

But we have another choice than to live this way. We can experiment with another possibility, the possibility that this moment, *exactly as it is*, is actually enough.

Don't just consider this mentally; consider it experientially. Let yourself feel into this possibility, the possibility that this moment is the miracle we've been seeking. After all, the fact that this moment even exists at all is truly beyond comprehension. Without asking or demanding anything from our momentary experience, without insisting it be better, more profound, more fulfilling, or more anything, see if you don't discover a depth and profundity, a richness and fulfillment that has always been here—here, *in this very instant,* the only one we will ever have.

Let this be not a one-time discovery but an ongoing, ever-deepening realization in your life.

Interpreting the World

What we call "reality" is really an interpretation the organism is rendering about whatever is being experienced. Quite literally, the world—at least the names we give it—is imagined.

But when I say imagined, I don't mean to suggest that the world is not real. Imagined simply refers to the fact that what we call reality is a translation or description of moment-to-moment phenomenal experience. We don't see the world as it is; we see our interpretation or translation of it.

And yet the funny thing is, all our words, all our interpretations, all our descriptions of what appears can never quite capture what is here. To be sure, we have our many labels that attempt to characterize the distinctive ways that life in its infinite variety and creativity patterns itself—self, flower, sky, anger, joy, tree, hunger, desire. But really, what are these things beyond their labels? Can we really capture any aspect of life in a word?

Try it right now. Can you really characterize any aspect of reality, actually put it into a definitive descriptive framework? Or are you just pretending to know what each momentary experience actually is?

Let the Moment Reveal Its Secrets

How is it that we know what anything actually is? Who told us a thought is a thought, fear is fear, joy is joy, a sensation is a sensation? What is the source of all this apparent certainty and knowledge we've come to? Who are the authorities we're deferring to—and *why* are we deferring to them—when we decide, "Oh, *this* is what this is?" Do we believe we know what things are because our parents told us so or because science says it's so? Or, are we saying this is the way it is because it's been written down in some scripture or uttered by some supposedly awakened person to be *the truth?*

Why do we rely on particular authorities to tell us how it is? Just listen to the seemingly endless stream of spiritual teachers throughout history—and now quite visible in the land of social media—discussing, dialoguing, debating, and sometimes arguing vociferously about what "reality" is and how best to realize it: "You must see through the self. There is no self to see through. Thought is the great deluder. Thought is empty of substance. There are many obstacles to realization. There are no obstacles. No effort is required to realize what you are. One must meditate every day to recognize the truth. Awakening is just the beginning. There is no such thing as awakening!" And on and on it goes . . .

But, for a moment, without deferring to anything or anyone, can we simply look and encounter what's here, nakedly and innocently, without referring to any outside authority to tell us what it is? Can we open ourselves in complete defenselessness and un-guardedness to what's here, allowing *experience itself* to tell us what it is, letting the moment reveal its secrets to us, freed from anyone else's ideas about what it might be or should be?

The Thread of Knowing

No matter how many practices we do or strategies we engage in, the only thing we will ever accomplish is to change our present experience.

Don't get me wrong—I like a pleasant experience as much as the next guy. But like you, every enjoyable, blissful or fulfilling experience I've ever managed to bring about has slipped away. Not a single one has remained.

But we have another choice: rather than trying to change the present moment into something we imagine will be better (or make us happier), we can simply recognize the thread of knowing that is woven through and ultimately inseparable from *all* experience.

Something is awake to, and knowing, *every* experience. Something is here, lighting up each and every moment. Recognize this knowing power that pervades everything, this presence that shines within every thought, every feeling, every sensation, and every circumstance. There is no need to create or conjure or cultivate this power; it is effortlessly present and inescapable.

See that experience is inseparable from the thread of knowing. The two cannot be pulled apart. They depend on one another. We don't need to seek after the light of knowing-awareness as some particular experience separate from other experiences. Instead, we can simply see that just as the warmth is inseparable from the sun, everything that appears experientially is inseparable from the light of knowing that reveals it.

Letting the River Flow

If one likens the flow of moment-to-moment experience to a river, trying to alter or stop the water's course simply ends up creating tension and discomfort and uses up considerable time, resources and energy.

But by allowing the river of experience to move and flow as it does (a flow we're really powerless to stop anyway), we increasingly discover an ease and comfort that is naturally present and available within and as the flow of experiencing itself.

Allowing our thoughts, feelings and sensations to be as they are does not, however, represent some kind of passivity or escape from the difficulties and challenges of life. In fact, letting the river of experience be *as it is* actually empowers us to meet everything in our lives more fully, more vulnerably, more openly, and more wisely.

This Precious Opportunity

In every moment we're given a fresh opportunity, uncolored by whatever may have come before, to recognize the miracle of life itself, to feel ourselves *as* the miracle of existence itself, this raw aliveness that is effortlessly present in and inseparable from every experience.

True, this light of awareness is always shining, unobstructed. But it's only in the *recognition* of it that its qualities of openness, of clarity, and of love begin to come more alive in our own direct experience.

Over and over again, life—through us—affords itself this fresh opportunity to see and revel in its own alive, awake nature. In every moment, this choice is always ours to make, this choice to recognize the miracle that stands before and as us, *right now.*

Searching for Rain in a Monsoon

Notice that awareness, the basic knowing of this moment, is already present. The activity of awareness is occurring effortlessly.

Now try to become unaware. Try to shut off the light switch of awareness. Notice that it's not really possible to turn off the knowing of this moment.

In many of the world's spiritual traditions, we're often instructed to become more present and aware. But in many ways, looking for the presence of awareness is a bit like searching for rain in a monsoon. It is unnecessary for you are already wet, saturated with the light of knowing, through and through.

We may look for awareness. But the reality is that it has been present at every step of the journey for it is awareness that's looking! And so the path is not so much about finding awareness as growing accustomed to the fact that it cannot disappear.

Rest in that, in the reality that awareness cannot go anywhere, the light of its sun, impossible to extinguish.

Expressing What Is

Allow yourself, right now, just to sit, not in order to obtain or acquire something, not so you can achieve a particular insight, experience, or state of mind, but for no other reason than to express what is.

Allow your practice, whatever it is, to be an *expression* of freedom, an expression of life, an expression of God rather than a means to realize it.

Describing

As humans, we have this remarkable capacity to describe our experiences. But what's fascinating is that we can't really pull it off, at least not completely. Try it right now; try to describe what is here experientially and tell me if you can ever truly or completely capture the present moment. You can't *really* do it, can you?

The reality is that whatever we describe about our selves or the world, it can only ever be a memory of what was here a moment ago. Life is simply too dynamic, too fleeting, too wild and free to ever really be captured by any of our words.

Deeply consider this, the impossibility of ever adequately describing the miracle that is each moment.

Naturally at Rest

Life is naturally at rest. It is never opposed to itself, never arguing with itself, never struggling with itself—for it is itself!

There is only life. And you are inseparably, indivisibly that.

So, rest naturally as that which you are: life itself, this life that is moving as all things, awake as all things.

Rest as the vastness of life, this totality that is always and already resting, naturally and effortlessly, not accepting all things but being all things.

Everything Vanishes Naturally

How remarkable it is that everything keeps slipping through our fingers, that every experience vanishes, just like that. What's here right now, gone. Poof! Vanished into thin air, each sensation dissolving into the next. Yesterday we had thousands of different thoughts and feelings. Where are they all now? All of them, up in smoke!

Each instant is completely fresh, completely new, even if in its newness, it is experienced as being somehow familiar, a recognizable pattern of perception. *"Oh yeah, I've seen this tree before, heard that song before, smelled that rose before . . ."* But actually we haven't. Not completely. We've never tasted this particular moment before. And we will never taste it again. For nothing is truly static; everything is on the move, forever shape-shifting into the next "thing." And yet, there really are no solid things because what we call a "thing" is really just a ceaseless flow of sensation, an ever-changing river of experiencing, impossible to really pin down and define.

So enjoy this impossibility of ever making any experience or insight stay in place. It simply cannot be done. The river keeps on flowing, moving and changing. It is impossible to stop and not necessary to stop, impossible to control and not necessary to control. We can just let the disappearing happen of its own accord, feeling the great release as each experience vanishes naturally and becomes what's next.

Natural Wakefulness

Life is awake in us, naturally and effortlessly. Somehow, the light switch of awareness is turned on and here we are, awake in and as the miracle of sentience shining through every moment.

Feel the stream of knowing that flows through every experience. It's like a warm presence shining within and illuminating every thought, feeling, and sensation. You need not create or cultivate this knowing; it is effortlessly present and inescapable.

Sense the awakeness of this life that is in you, this life that is you. Rest in this natural wakefulness that you are, revel in it, bask in its warmth, enjoying and living as the openheartedness that touches and is touched by everything.

No Need to Strive

Relax body and mind completely,
there is nothing to find.

Relax body and mind completely,
there is nothing that binds.

Relax body and mind completely,
there is nothing to know.

Relax body and mind completely,
there is nothing to grasp hold of, or let go.

Relax body and mind completely,
there is no need to strive.

Relax body and mind completely,
there is no place to arrive.

Relax body and mind completely,
there is nothing to defend.

Relax body and mind completely,
there is nothing to overcome
or transcend.

This Unavoidable Intimacy

Much of the internal suffering we experience stems from our efforts to try to escape what is arising. Our attempts to control our thoughts, feelings, and sensations in order to find a sense of freedom, ease, and well-being invariably end up creating more tension and stress, a sense of being divided, alienated from ourselves and from life. It is, in a very real sense, like waging war against our selves, this effort to escape our own experience, this struggle with *what is*.

And yet, the truth is that we can't actually pull it off; despite our best, most sincere efforts, we simply aren't able to escape our present-moment experience. We may try to keep certain experiences at bay, try to shield or defend ourselves against the onslaught of life. But the reality is that no matter how hard we may try to barricade ourselves from our own experience, we never actually succeed in creating separation or distance. In the end, there really is no pulling ourselves out of or away from whatever is being thought, felt, or sensed.

There is no fleeing the here-and-now but only ever this unavoidable intimacy with what is.

Embracing Uncertainty

What will happen today? Who will I meet? What events will take place?

And what about the next thought, the next feeling, the next sensation? What will it bring? Fear, happiness, sadness, joy, boredom, excitement? It is all quite uncertain and unpredictable, isn't it?

But not only is the future unknowable. The present moment is also filled with considerable uncertainty. Sure, we have great knowledge about our inner and outer worlds. We have many names for whatever is being seen, heard, felt, touched, or tasted in any moment. But look at any of the descriptive labels we apply to experience and see if there is any real certainty about what those labels actually mean. Take fear . . . Do we really know what fear is? We have a sense of what this thing called fear is, enough so that we've come up with a name for it and seem able to communicate about the experience to others with some shared sense of understanding what it is that's being spoken about. But again, can we say, with any real conviction or certainty that we know what fear truly is?

We might say fear is a kind of clenching, a feeling of constriction or tightness in the body coupled with a pattern of thinking that seems to be focused on concerns about what might or might not happen. But let's break that description down and really look at it. What are those sensations, actually? What is "tightness" or "constriction"? Go beyond the labels and just experience the raw sensations themselves, very directly. What is there, experientially? Sure, we have a word for it—sensation. But do we even know what that word means? What are sensations made of?

We can ask the same about thoughts too. We use this

word, "thought" to describe a certain type or category of experience. And we assume at some level that we know what a thought is. But do we, *really?*

Now, when it comes to the experience labeled as fear, the neuroscientist might argue, *"Oh, we have a pretty good idea what fear is and where it is located in the brain."* They might even tell you that at some point, we'll be able to pinpoint very precisely, the exact neuronal activity that is responsible for fear. But even at this more concrete level, when we look at what makes up these things called the "body" and "brain" that are supposedly responsible for the arising of fear, our certainty very quickly begins to fade for the farther we go into the nature of the body and brain itself (cellularly, molecularly, sub-atomically), the deeper we venture into very unknown and very uncertain terrain.

Of course the spiritual philosopher/sage might answer the question of what fear is by saying that it is merely the play of consciousness or universal intelligence. They might even proclaim such things as self-evident truths and do so with a great, seemingly absolute level of certainty and conviction. But when one says that fear is consciousness, what are they actually saying? For just as we did with the sensations and thoughts that constitute the fear experience, we can do the same with the label, "consciousness."

Look and ask yourself, *"What is consciousness?"* Scientists and mystics alike throw the word around a lot. But do any of us really know what it is? When the spiritual teacher proclaims that, *"all is consciousness,"* what are they actually saying? It sounds like they know what they're talking about, that they're quite certain about it all. But are they? Can we really be so certain that we know what this word consciousness is even pointing to? Or could it be that we're simply taking such proclamations as a matter of faith (or perhaps hope?). Whether we inquire more objectively or subjectively into a state such as fear (or the consciousness that is its supposed basis), we're still left not really knowing, uncertain, in the end, about exactly what these labels of fear and consciousness are even pointing to.

Of course, this is one of the central functions of language, to create conceptual maps and linguistic categories that help us label and navigate the world of experience. However, if we start imagining our conceptual interpretations to be the final truths about the "way things are," then we will end up with the very rigidity, close-mindedness, and political, philosophical and religious intolerance that have plagued us as a species for so many thousands of years. For if we assume we already know and are quite certain about life and the phenomena that constitute it, then we effectively close ourselves off to learning and discovering anything new, certain that we already know what experiences are simply because we have words to describe them: *"Oh, I know what that experience is, it's fear . . . or it's happiness . . . that thing over there, oh yeah that's a tree . . . and that's a bird sitting in it . . . "*

If, however, we can begin to see that our descriptions are really interpretive renderings of life rather than definitive statements about it's nature, we can begin to hold our knowledge much more lightly, much less rigidly. We can live both in the knowing and certainty of things as well as the not knowing and uncertainty of them. As the Zen saying goes, "first there is a mountain, then there is no mountain, then there is . . . " Yes, we know that mountains are mountains. We have a name for that object of perception. We "know" what it is. But if we really look (whether experientially or analytically) at what constitutes this thing called, a mountain, we can begin to appreciate that we don't really know what a mountain (or anything else for that matter) *actually* is, even if at one level we do. This is the paradox. That we know what things are, but we also don't . . .

What if instead of running from and defending against the uncertainty inherent in existence, we actually embraced it? What if we allowed ourselves that much vulnerability, opened ourselves to the incredible unknowability of it all? Are we willing to see that our stories and interpretations of reality are just that, stories and interpretations rather than statements of fact about the way things are? If we adopt some framework of understanding (a religion, a theory, a philosophy) to try to make sense of our human experience, can we at least admit to ourselves and the world that these are just frameworks rather than imagining them to be the final gospel or truth? Can we learn to live with the reality of this great uncertainty that is staring us in the face at every turn, embrace that uncertainty, and in so doing, open ourselves to the unending mystery of everything?

No Effort to Maintain

Here's a very simple yet powerful meditation . . . Simply sit and make no effort to maintain or hold in place any experience that might arise . . . That's it.

Acceptance

There is quite a bit of talk in psychological and spiritual circles these days about becoming more accepting, of our selves and our experience. But in many ways, acceptance isn't really something we do so much as a description of the way things actually *are.*

What do I mean? Well, life we could say, is by its very nature accepting for life is never opposed to itself, never set apart from or in resistance to any of its manifestations, much as the ocean is never in opposition to any of its waves. The ocean can neither accept nor reject the waves for it *is* not separate from them. The waves are its expression.

While we may seek to *love what is,* the truth is that what's here is already loved. What's here is already accepted, *already* welcomed, without question or reason. Otherwise, how could it have arisen?

So, for a moment, don't try to accept what is here but simply see that life has already allowed this experience to be as it is for life *is* experience.

Let the acceptance of what is be this natural, this effortless, for it is the nature of life, the nature of you to be so.

Relax

Relax.

Relax all effort
and allow the ceaseless flow
of experience to unfold,
as it unfolds,
to arise as it arises,
to flower and to subside,
in its own time
and its own rhythm.

Relax into what is.

Relax into
the flow
of thinking,
relax
into the flow
of feeling,
relax
into the flow
of awareness
that knows both
thinking and feeling.

Relax
into
whatever
is here . . .

Hearts without Skin

For a moment, just sense into your own existence, the simple *feeling of being*. Now imagine that there is nothing standing between you and the world, nothing separating this raw, vulnerable, naked aliveness that you are from the whole of life. Even the skin that we sometimes imagine, even if subtly, to be serving as a kind of barrier between us and the world is made *of* the world.

We are completely exposed. There is no protection, nothing actually shielding us from life. We are like hearts without skin—utterly vulnerable, touched by everything, permeable membranes, freely mixing with life, inseparable from life.

Ironically, it is the attempt to protect or defend our psychological selves that creates the sense of not being safe in the first place. Put another way, in allowing ourselves to be totally vulnerable, we come to find a profound invulnerability, the discovery that experiences cannot harm us because they are not separate from us. As *The Course in Miracles* so beautifully says, "In my defenselessness, my safety lies . . . "

So, make no effort to keep away this incredible openheartedness. You can't do it anyway! Revel in it, marinate in the heart's nakedness. Be this utter vulnerability that you are, already. A heart without skin . . .

The River of Experience

Like a river, the experiences of life are a constant, uninterrupted and unimpeded flow of dynamic change and flux. Nothing really stands still. The river of life never really stops long enough to be captured by our descriptions. It's simply too dynamic, too creative for that.

Whether it's external events or our internal thoughts, feelings and sensations, whatever we are describing has actually already moved on, even if we imagine it's still here.

Life simply flows, a continuous, uninterrupted stream, a beauty that is quite literally beyond description, beyond any and all labels we might give it.

Where Is Awareness?

Resting comfortably, ask yourself, *"Are sounds being heard right now?"* Notice that sounds are being registered effortlessly, that *something,* we know not what exactly, is hearing. Sounds are being experienced.

Rest as the knowing of sound. Rest as the experiencing of sound. Rest as the awareness that is aware of sound.

Now ask yourself, with eyes open, *"Are sights being seen?"* Notice that visual images are being registered, effortlessly.

Rest as that which sees. Rest as the seeing itself. Rest as that which knows each image that appears.

Feel the sense of touch, the point of contact between your body and whatever surface the body sits or stands upon. Feel the sense of air touching skin. Notice that these sensations are being registered, effortlessly.

Rest as the noticing of sensation, rest as the sense of touching, and being touched.

Relax as the knowing that is aware of each experience, aware of each sound, each sight, and each touch. There is no need to search for this basic knowing. It is already the case.

Rest as that . . .

This Timeless Moment

Notice that what we call *this moment* flows without ceasing. There is never an interruption.

Now, look into your experience and ask: *"Can I find a clear line separating this moment from what was or what will be?"*

Everything Slips Away

What's here, right now—the particular constellation of thoughts, feelings, sensations, and perceptions being experienced—is it appearing or disappearing? Isn't the arising of each instant also its passing away? Try to keep what's here from slipping away. It can't be done. No experience, no realization, no insight can ever be held in place. Life, the eternal shape shifter.

It's really not possible for us to hold on to anything; we're powerless to stop this ceaseless and spontaneous arising and passing away of phenomena.

Every instant of life, each momentary flash of experience, vanishes without a trace. All that exists is this immediacy, a here-and-now that can never actually be captured or contained, for no sooner does it appear than it's gone.

We speak of "holding on" and "letting go," but really, what's here can never be held on to *or* released. What we call the moment has already taken flight long before we ever try to do anything about it.

Sky Mind

As you sit here, you may be seeing many things. But regardless of what is being seen within or without, simply rest as the seeing itself, the space from where you are looking.

Feel into that space. *Be* that space. Feel the endless openness of it. Sense that it has no edges or borders to it.

The looking is like the sky—vast, spacious, completely open, rejecting nothing, allowing everything. You *are* this cloudless sky that sees.

Rest as that, allowing whatever weather patterns of experience may appear, to appear. Feel the loving, welcoming nature of this open sky, this sky that can resist no cloud.

Thought

It's ironic that "thought," the very thing that seems to drive so much of our lives actually has no tangible substance. We can't see thoughts, can't hold them in our hands. And yet, thoughts seem to influence us in ways that nothing else does! Isn't that something?

Let's take one thought, maybe the big daddy of them all as it is the source of so much human suffering: *"this experience should be other than it is . . ."* What is that thought, really? Where is it? Can you find the thought? Where does it come from and where does it go when it leaves? And, what is thought even made of? How is it that something that really isn't a thing at all, can both move, and torment us in all the many ways it does? Isn't that remarkable, the power that has been granted something that we can't even see, touch, taste or hear?

The more we contemplate the unfindable, insubstantial nature of thought and the irony that despite this, it is still seemingly able to exert such power and influence over our lives, the more it begins to dawn on us just how free we actually are from thought, how able we are to move in the direction thought may be pointing, or not, free to listen to its guidance or not, to follow its ways or not, to imagine it speaks some truth or not, or to believe in its authority or not.

After all, it's not as if thought is some terrorist with a gun to our heads saying, *"You'd better walk this way or else . . ."* It's just a thought! Where is the threat, actually? Where is the power? Thought is nothing but a swirl of imagery, a flickering of ungraspable energy. Thought is evanescent, ephemeral, invisible. It has no power of its own, save that which we grant it.

Pick your favorite thought nemesis: *"I should be better at*

this than I am . . ." "This moment isn't satisfying enough . . ."
"I should be more like that person;" "I should be happier, more
aware, more peaceful . . ." "Something terrible will happen if
they disapprove of me . . ." Can you see how insubstantial
and empty all these thoughts are and how free you are because of this?

It is quite humbling to recognize just how much of our
lives—from what we imagine we should be doing, to how
we believe we should be doing it, to who we believe we are
or ought to be . . . all of it built on this flimsy, ephemeral
wisp of nothing we call, thought. It is liberating indeed to
see through the illusion of almighty thought, to recognize
that it is not the be all, end all gospel of truth we so often
imagine it to be, not the final word on anything.

Just stop and notice, right now, how insubstantial
thought is and how it has no actual power to do anything
in this moment. Thought is not your commander, not your
captor, not your ruler, not your terrorizer. In fact, it's really nothing at all, nothing, but empty space, through and
through—impossible to find, impossible to grasp hold of.
How can something that cannot even be found or seen or
located have any true power to tell you what you are or who
you must be; to dictate to you what life is or how it ought to
appear in this moment?

Separation

Often what drives us to take up various therapeutic or spiritual practices is the sense that we are somehow separate—separate and apart from our selves, from each other, and from life . . .

For a moment, just feel into this sense of being separate, the feeling that you somehow stand apart from life, disconnected from the whole. Really feel into it, the sense of being isolated and alone. Hold nothing back from fully feeling this sense of separation. Experience it, completely.

Now ask yourself, in the actual felt sense of this experience we label as "separation," can you actually find any separation there? Can you find a boundary, a clear line dividing "you" from "not you," or separating "in here" from "out there?"

Try to locate it. Try to find evidence for this thing called, "separation." Where is it? Can you clearly point to separation and say, "There, there it is!" Can you find evidence of a beginning, middle, or end to this thing called, separation? Or, when you go to look for it, do you come up empty-handed?

Look into the sense of separation and see if you can find anything there but vivid, wide-open, borderless awareness, the lifeblood of everything.

This Mighty Flame

Notice that no matter your experience, the fire of awareness is already lit and burning brightly, illuminating and making known, whatever is being experienced. The whole world is on fire, a mighty blaze of knowing burning wildly out of control, its flames dancing as a million different sparks of experience.

Now, don't merely notice this wild, fiery display that is always and already burning. Don't keep yourself apart from its flames, watching them as if from some far off, distant place. No, see that you *are* this burning, that it is *you* who are on fire, and that no experience can ever extinguish this mighty flame.

Awareness, Just This

Consider the possibility that every sensation, whether described as desirable or undesirable, pleasurable or painful, is none other *than* awareness.

Consider the possibility that awareness is not some "thing" watching some other thing, not a "subject" observing happy or sad, peaceful or disturbing "objects." Awareness *pervades* what is seen. In fact, see if you can find any line separating what knows—i.e., awareness—from whatever is being known. That which perceives is inseparable from what it perceives, is it not?

There isn't disturbance or discomfort on the one hand and the ever-present peace of awareness on the other. Awareness is inseparable from all mind states. If you want to know what awareness is, it's quite simple. *It's whatever is being experienced, right now!* And so, from that vantage, there is no possibility of ever entering or leaving awareness.

What is awareness? Just this . . . and this . . . and this . . .

Something Is Always Being Seen

Seeing is always happening. Something is *always* being seen, even if what is being seen is a sense that something is missing, that what is being seen is somehow, not quite enough.

Regardless of what might be arising experientially or how we might label it—pleasant, unpleasant, clear, confused, ordinary, or extraordinary—the seeing is always here, right at the center of it all. The seeing can never be absent because everything that appears, appears to the seeing. Everything is illumined by that invisible light . . .

In fact, everything is that light, the seeing none other than the seen. Never absent. Always present. And always, only ever, *right now*.

Freedom Is Not a Particular Experience

In a dream, I saw myself meditating. I heard myself, as the meditator, say: *"Awareness makes everything possible. Nothing would exist without awareness. That's why I place my attention there rather than on the particulars of experience; that's why I'm devoted to awareness—because nothing is more important than this capacity we have to know each and every experience."*

But then, I heard another voice: *"Yes, but without experience, without the content or the particulars, you would never know awareness."*

The voice went on: *"Awareness is not a 'thing' separate from other things. Awareness is not merely this clear, untouched space witnessing or knowing thoughts, feelings, sensations, sights, sounds, colors . . . Awareness is shining as those things."*

We cannot find awareness apart from the particular textures of our experience. It's inseparable from all the flavors of life. Awareness is not found or located as some "particular" separate from other "particulars." It is *all* particulars. We don't have to seek it out. We don't have to look for awareness because it is already being given, *right now,* as whatever is happening experientially. Everything is this illumination, everything this vividness, everything this bright knowing. Everything. Nothing is left out of this love. Nothing.

No Need to Keep Track

If you've ever practiced meditation, you may have noticed this tendency to try to track where you are, to keep looking at your experience in order to gauge how you're doing, to find out whether or not the state you are in is the right or correct state.

But for this moment, consider the possibility that there is really nothing to keep track of, no distractions to pull your self away from, or correct state to get yourself into.

Maybe, just maybe, it is *all* the play of life, a vast and open field with no point of entry or escape.

Resting as Awareness

When you "rest as awareness" there's no need to engage in some activity or mental exercise in order to make yourself more aware. To rest is to simply see that awareness—*that which knows this moment*—requires no cause or effort for it to be.

Notice that you can never find a time when the light of knowing is switched off, for everything that appears—each flashing thought and feeling, every sensation and perception—is the vivid proof that awareness is already here. See that no matter how you may try to move or manipulate the mind, awareness remains itself, aware.

So, rest this weary mind and see that no amount of doing will ever bring you closer to its light, the light of awareness that's always and already blazing like a million suns.

Points of View

There is no completely clear or "perspective-free" zone. That's a fantasy. We can only ever see our point of view, a moment-to-moment translation the organism is making of this whirling, swirling sea of energy and mystery we call life.

In each instant, incalculable bits of information/sensory data are being processed and we, as organisms, come to the conclusion that the particular constellation of data points being experienced is, in fact, equal to whatever particular name we may be giving it . . . body . . . self . . . fear . . . happiness . . .

And while making such interpretations is natural, what's crucial is to see that we are actually doing this, that what we call, "reality" is very much an interpretation, that our experiences (of our selves and the world), are renderings rather than facts.

Look into your experience, right now, and ask: *"Is there any holding on to the particular points of view that are arising? Am I imagining this interpretation the body-mind is making to represent some sort of 'truth' or final word about the way things are?"*

"Can I recognize that life is being interpreted and as a result, begin to hold all of it much more lightly? Can I see that no matter how sophisticated my language might be or how remarkable this capacity to interpret and describe the myriad expressions and forms that life takes, life remains, in its essence, a mystery?"

"Can I also see that if I am unable to laugh about my interpretations or points of view, no matter how seemingly wise, true or sophisticated they might appear to me (or even others), it's probably a pretty good sign I've become identified with those points of view?"

Reality

There is
no escaping
Reality,
no entering
or leaving,
no matter
how much
we may imagine
that we can.

Everything is
as it is,
Reality,
in harmony
with itself—
wind being wind,
rain being rain,
fear being fear . . .

We may argue
with Reality,
struggle with what is,
but we will forever
lose that quarrel
only to find ourselves
shattered and in tears.
And then that, too,
will be Reality.

The Center

Relax into whatever is being experienced. Now ask yourself, *"What is at the center of this experience?"*

Don't attempt to answer that question conceptually. Simply explore it experientially. *"What is the felt sense of this that lies at the center of my experience, however that experience might be described?"*

You might feel as if there is a self there, i.e., a "you." If so, go deeper . . . what is at the center of that, the center of this self you call, you? Again, don't try to answer the question mentally; answer it experientially. What is at the center? How does it feel? What's it shape? It's texture?

Maybe your answer is that at the center of this experience is a sense of presence, a sense of being aware. Great. Now ask yourself, *"What is at the center of that? What lies at the center of this presence of awareness being sensed?"*

Maybe you find nothing there, nothing but a sense of wide-open empty space. Perfect. Then ask your self once more, *"What lies there, here in the center of this empty, open space?"*

There is no end to this inquiry.

Just enjoy the endlessness of it . . .

What You're Searching For

Whatever it is you feel you are searching for—love, peace, freedom, happiness . . . for a moment, just pick your favorite word and consider this: Every experience is *that*.

Let's say it's freedom that you desire. Just sit here and relax into *what is*. Relax into whatever is arising experientially.

As you do this, rather than employing some strategy to remove yourself from what is being experienced in order to find what you desire, in this example, "freedom," just consider that your present experience is *already* freedom, that each thought, feeling and sensation is the movement and activity of freedom itself.

Consider that there is no entering some state, called freedom nor any possibility of ever exiting it. There is *only* freedom, appearing as each momentary arising, manifesting as each stirring of life.

The Force of Life

All the states we've ever tried to avoid or change into some-thing else—the anger, the fear, the insecurity, the confusion, the anxiety—simply by relaxing and allowing those experiences to be exactly as they are, we can discover that every one of them, left uncorrected, is actually the seat of the most tremendous power and energy, the fuel and force of the whole cosmos.

Simply allow this moment to be that powerful, to be the immense force of life that it is has always been.

Identification

Is it possible that life isn't actually capable of collapsing into any identity other than itself?

Could it be that the sentience and intelligence of life never really "loses itself" in anything other than its own awake nature?

After all, what is it that grasps, and then lets go of grasping, that seemingly identifies and then lets go of identification?

Maybe it is this permanence that is forever changing, the flame of reality that dances and flickers a thousand different ways and yet is always only burning . . .

The Looking Is Loving

That which sees this moment loves this moment, without condition. Just look, and you'll see that the looking is not capable of rejecting whatever is being seen.

Now ask yourself, is the seeing of this moment separate from this moment? Or is the seeing itself, indivisible from that which is seen?

Can you find a line dividing what appears and the seeing of it? Or, is there only ever the seamlessness of life, dancing as both the subject seeing and objects that are seen?

Always Looking

We may seek to find awareness but the truth is, we can't escape it for awareness is always here.

Look at the ground beneath your feet and awareness is there, gazing from your eyes.

Turn your attention to the sky above and awareness is still there.

Gaze within and see your thoughts and feelings and again, there is awareness, noticing the vast galaxies of experience swirling within.

We don't create awareness for it is already here. And we can't really make it go away, either. Awareness simply is.

It takes no effort to be aware. All you have to do is bring a little attention to it, just notice that awareness is effortlessly and spontaneously present and then allow your self to relax into its open, spacious arms and then see how the world looks from that place, the very place you've always been looking from.

Let the Birds Fly

Allow the birds of thought, feeling and sensation to fly wherever they may fly. Make no effort to control their ever-changing, unpredictable course and flight.

Feel as if you are this vast sky in which the birds are flying, so wild and free, the sky in which the world of experience appears, then disappears, just like that.

Now ask yourself, *"Can I find any separation between the sky and what appears in the sky? Could it be that everything in the sky is made up of sky? Or, maybe the sky is made up of everything that appears within it?"*

Is it possible that everything we experience is but an expression of a vast and boundless field of knowing, itself invisible, yet visible as everything that appears?"

Something Knows

The reality is that both the wonderful and horrible, the expansive and contracted, the most illuminating and most troubling experiences are all gone now. Every insight that has ever appeared has now disappeared. And yet the appearing and disappearing were known by *something*, were they not? Every joy, every sorrow, every moment of clarity and confusion has appeared to . . . something, right?

Something has known each and every arising and passing away. There is something here that knows each moment, whether the moment is appearing as ordinary or extraordinary, boring or exciting, awake or asleep.

Simply rest in that which knows, whatever or wherever that may be. This bright awareness cannot be found or located as a separate, clearly definable "thing." And yet its presence cannot be denied either.

Bowing to the Mystery

We don't actually know how life, and the awareness of it, is coming about.

We really have no idea how this moment is able even to be here, how anything is happening at all!

What is left, then, but to bow in the face of this vast and incomprehensible mystery, a mystery that is so much greater than us, even as it is what we are, through and through?

Impermanence

Observe your experience—how long does it actually last? The present sensation that is arising—is it here for a nanosecond, or perhaps even less?

Can you locate any experience that doesn't disappear as soon as it appears?

All the names we give to these fleeting phenomena—are we naming what is actually here or are we only ever describing what was, a memory that somehow lingers, like an echo?

Can we really describe experience? Or is it simply too dynamic ever to be captured by a word?

Amazing, isn't it?

Mind Swallowed

All is quiet now—
the sun of certainty
has set.
Only night remains,
the dark and
haunting silence
that swallows mind
and with it,
what we call
"the world."

Flying Airplanes into Buildings

September 11th, among many other things, can serve as a powerful reminder about the madness that ensues when we hold to any of our points of view as if our lives depended on them.

Just ask yourself, *"How many times have I (metaphorically speaking) been willing to fly airplanes into buildings or blow things up simply to prove the rightness of my point of view or defend it as "true"?*

No Adequate Translation

This momentary flash of experience can never be adequately captured, contained, or understood with any of our linguistic or conceptual frameworks. Not really.

We may have many names for the different patterns and swirls of life energy appearing and then disappearing. But what is anything, really? Take any word—light, sound, self, fear, joy, bird, warmth, confusion, awareness—what are these, not as ideas but as experiences? We can't *really* say, can we?

Even though our words and names give us the impression we know what this worded world actually is, we really don't. Check it out—try to define *this* momentary flash of experience and you'll quickly see it isn't really possible. There is no adequate translation nor interpretation that will really suffice.

It's like a great fireworks display, moment by moment, this explosion of life—unpredictable, unmanageable, uncontrollable, and undefinable. But when we relax this habit of trying to manage, control or define it, we begin to discover how profound, how awe inspiring, how miraculous everything is in its indescribability. And the more we realize that "what is" cannot actually be contained by any word, any model, any theory or description, no matter how seemingly true or sublime they may be, the more there is a natural sense of open-heartedness, flexibility, and clarity that pervades the whole of our life.

Constellations of Experience

When we look up into the clear night sky, we see a vast array of twinkling lights. Some of these stars seem to form distinct patterns or shapes that, over the centuries, we have come to name—The Big Dipper, Orion's Belt, Capricorn the Goat, Sagittarius the Archer.

But is there really something out there that *is* The Big Dipper, something that actually exists? Or is there just a recognizable patterning of stars to which we've given the name, "The Big Dipper"? In a very real sense, we can see that there really is no such thing as a Big Dipper. It is a construction, an invention of mind. Mind has, quite literally, brought the Big Dipper into existence by virtue of having named it!

Constellations in the night sky are a very powerful metaphor for the myriad ways we name, categorize, label and describe what are essentially patterns of phenomenal experience. Fear, anxiety, joy, worry, jealousy, excitement—look and see if these states of mind are, like constellations, simply recognizable patterns of phenomena that we have learned to label in particular ways. Really, there is no such thing as anxiety any more than there is a Big Dipper. There is just a certain pattern of phenomenal experience we have grown accustomed to describing as, "anxiety." Like constellations, mental-emotional states are constructions of mind, literally brought into existence by virtue of the names given them.

To recognize this is to begin to find greater freedom in the midst of all these mental constellations we've imagined ourselves to be the victims of. For what once appeared to be fixed constellations of experience, are now seen for what they are—a dynamic, ungraspable flow and patterning of life, twinkling stars in the night sky of experience.

Wordlessly Alive

This moment, appearing
then disappearing—
is it ever really here
long enough to be called
some thing?
Or is there only ever
this shimmering river
of sensation
that flows
without ceasing—
never stopping,
never freezing,
never holding still
long enough
to be named.
Wordlessly alive,
beyond all possibility
of ever being known,
yet brightly knowing.

Abandon Yourself

Abandon yourself to worry
and you will discover
what has never known fear.

Surrender yourself to insecurity
and you will find
what has always been safe.

Give yourself over to bondage
and you will find
what has always been liberated.

Disappear into contraction
and you will see
what has never been closed.

Submit yourself to separation
and you will find
what has remained
forever undivided.

Come Rest

Come rest here,
here in this thought,
this feeling, this moment
of great sorrow or joy.

Come rest, here in the sounds
of children laughing
and the anguished cries
of those who imagine
they've lost their way.

Come rest, here,
here in the cradle
of a warm summer night,
and the blistering cold
of winter's dawn.

Come rest in this
for there is nowhere
else to rest.

The Great Unraveling

Notice that when experiences are left unrejected and unaltered, they unravel themselves naturally, without effort or struggle. This is the unstoppably dynamic nature of everything.

No matter how hard we may try to sustain or eliminate an experience, it will vanish of its own accord for that is its nature, to not remain the same.

Let this inescapable truth sink in deeply. See that regardless of our efforts to either allow or alter our experience, thoughts, feelings, sensations and the awareness that illumines them are forever undoing themselves, moment by timeless moment.

This Welcoming Sky

You are
the embrace
of everything,
the vast sky-like
nature of mind
that refuses no cloud,
that welcomes
both sun and rain.

Radical Embrace

Throughout history, humans have engaged in many practices in order to go beyond whatever they've found too painful—denial, avoidance, rejection, dissociation, drugs—as well as various spiritual methods aimed at realizing a freedom and ease beyond the world of form, experience, and phenomena.

But another choice exists, a path not of beyond-ness or transcendence but of what we might call "radical embrace." In this path, the diagnosis of what ails us may be the same, namely that our discontent is the result of grasping after particular experiences, imagining that those experiences (and not others) will bring us the happiness and well-being we've been seeking.

But instead of rejecting or attempting to get beyond experiences and the world, in the path of radical embrace, we discover that freedom actually lies right in the heart of experience. In the path of radical embrace, we apply no effort to get beyond experience because we recognize this isn't really possible. There's no such thing as "beyond," no escape hatch, no way to be free of experience—because whatever we might call "beyond," once realized, immediately becomes the next thing that is known, i.e., the next experience.

The invitation in the path of radical embrace is to realize that every moment, every sensation, and every experience is actually home, that freedom doesn't lie in some realm beyond experiences. Such a realm exists only as an abstraction. True freedom exists in and as the very flow of experience itself. In this pathless path, there *is* no beyond; there is only ever what's here. And, left unrejected, what's here reveals itself to be the very freedom and love we've been seeking.

You Can't Stop the Wind

Relax . . .
You cannot make
the sun shine,
nor can you keep it
from shining.

Relax . . .

You are powerless
to accept or reject
this moment.
It's too late for that.
What is here
is already here.
Relax . . .

Nothing needs
to happen.

Your efforts to arrive
somewhere else
will not succeed,
for there is no escaping
the only thing there is.

Relax . . .

Life cannot hurt you,
for you are Life.

Being

When all efforts
to make something
else happen relax,
when all strategies
and techniques
to get beyond
the mind or self
have finally
exhausted
themselves,
it is seen that
no effort was ever
required to be,
though being
never refused
a single effort.

Something Is Here

Something
is here,
welcoming
everything
the mind
wishes
were not.

Rest as that
welcoming . . .

Resistance Is Futile

The truth of the matter is, we can never actually escape what's happening. It's not possible. We can't remove ourselves from what is because we *are* what is. Resistance is, as they say, futile.

So, that's the invitation on offer here, to see what happens when the battle is let go, to see what happens to "you" when the struggle with experience relaxes.

We suffer, quite literally, under the illusion that if we can somehow manage, modify, or control our experiences in a certain way, we will finally be happy, safe, awake, or free.

But what if it weren't true? What if experiences didn't require any manipulation or fixing? What if our thoughts, feelings and sensations didn't need to look or appear any particular way?

Sun of Awareness

The sunlight
of awareness
is not revealed
when the clouds
of doubt
and despair
part.

The sun
is revealed
in each and
every cloud,
its brilliance
shining within
all things.

Rest in,
and as
this ever
present
light.

No Match

All the strategies
we engage in
either to resist
or to accept what is—
they are like
throwing feathers
into a raging wind.
We are simply
no match for
the force of
this love.

The Secret

There is great fascination with discovering what "the secret" is, the key that will unlock all the riches we ever dreamed of, manifest all the relationships we've ever longed for, shower us with whatever fame, fortune, adoration, or enlightenment we imagine will bring us happiness.

But the real secret is to realize there is no secret, to see that nothing we could ever do, think, feel, find, obtain, or manifest will ever bring us what we truly desire. *The happiness we seek is what we've always been.* Fulfillment is our very nature, the nature of life itself. That's the secret. And no one can teach it, transmit it, or sell it to you.

The real secret is to see that this moment—*the very one appearing, right now*—is not, as the mind would have us believe, a means to some imagined end. This moment is the end, the endless miracle of just this.

This Miracle

We overlook
the miracle
that lies
before us
for the
simple reason
that we keep
looking for it
somewhere
else.

Simply Because It Is

When attention
begins to lose
its fascination
with the
mind's stories,
what remains
is the simple
wonder of this—
a crack in
the sidewalk,
the paper clip
on my desk,
a speck of dust
on the floor,
the rush of wind
through the trees—
everything is ablaze
with this quiet,
heart-wrenching beauty,
simply because it is.

Life, Forever Transcending Our Descriptions

Despite our remarkable capacity to label and describe the world within and around us, life cannot really be adequately captured or contained by any of our conceptual, philosophical, religious, or scientific frameworks, no matter how sophisticated or "true" they might appear.

Just try to find words to capture what breakfast tasted like this morning, what a beautiful sunset looks like, or how it feels to stub your toe, and you'll begin to see how each and every moment literally transcends any and all attempts to categorize or label it.

Too Swift to Capture

All futures, all pasts,
all dreams, all regrets,
all ideas and ideals,
vanished, swallowed up
in this quiet simplicity,
this mystery of now
that keeps exploding
into what's next,
this that is too alive
to ever be
held or fixed,
a bird of time
too swift
to capture.

Letting the Wind Blow

Imagine your thinking is like a wind. Sometimes it blows quite strongly, gusting with a mighty force and power.

Other times, it's more of a gentle breeze, a zephyr, the movement of air, barely perceptible or maybe even completely still.

Either way, as you sit here, make no effort to stop the wind from blowing. Whether howling or quiet, simply let the air dance, however it dances.

Let thinking blow like the wind, as freely and wildly and unpredictably as it does.

No need to control it. No need to try to slow it down. No need to keep the wind from blowing. You really can't anyway! Just let it move, however it wishes to move. Let the winds of thinking blow naturally and effortlessly.

Just as the air is not wrong for moving the way that it does, so too with the winds of thinking. Whatever direction they may blow is fine. However strongly the winds of mind might howl, make no effort to lessen their force or power.

Simply let the winds of mind blow. That is all . . .

The Power of Life

Reflect for a moment on the power of life. It's everywhere—the sun, the wind, the trillions of stars, volcanoes, butterflies, the human brain, an ant; the unfathomable number of sub-atomic particles swirling in and as everything.

In all that we see, there blazes such power, such intelligence, such magnificence. We are that same power. It is our nature and the nature of everything.

Nothing is ever separate.

The Body Is Conscious

For generations, scientists and philosophers have debated the matter of consciousness, arguing over whether it is dependent upon the body and brain for its existence or not. There are those who contend that consciousness exists in some way prior to or beyond the brain and that the body is essentially dependent upon it, whereas others believe that without the activity of the body-brain, there would simply be no consciousness. I won't attempt to resolve this age-old debate here. But in this meditation, I'd like to invite you to take up the latter position, even if for a brief moment, and consider that the body is giving rise to consciousness, rather than the other way around.

For a moment, simply feel into the dynamic activity of life we call *the body.* Sense the miracle of its very existence, the miracle of thinking, of feeling, of sensation. Notice how the body is giving rise to countless experiences and is doing so quite naturally and effortlessly. Hearing, seeing, sensing . . . see how the body is generating these, seemingly without our consent. Much as the rose naturally gives off its beautiful color and sweet perfume, the body is producing its own unique fragrances in the form of the myriad experiences and perceptions that arise in every moment.

Now notice awareness—the activity of *basic knowing* that is present and arising here, spontaneously. Through the remarkable activity of the body and brain and the billions of cells and probably trillions of molecules, atoms, electrons and subatomic particles that constitute the life of each cell, sentience is somehow miraculously arising. The body is awake and conscious, effortlessly. Just as the rose cannot help but give off its sweet smell, so too is the body producing the aroma of consciousness for it is its nature to do so.

Now feel into this configuration of life we call "the body" and see if you can find anything dividing the body from the totality of life. Sense how the body is but an extension of the boundlessness of existence itself. Consider this notion that the body is producing consciousness, that the body is giving off the fragrance of awareness as part of its natural functioning and ask: "Is it the body that is awake or is it the universe that is conscious?" For isn't the body inseparable from the universe, with no lines of division anywhere to be found?

Letting the Fire Burn

Imagine your feelings are like a fire. Maybe it's just a tiny flicker of a flame, like a little candle burning in the night. Or maybe it's like a wild brush fire, raging wildly out of control.

Either way, make no effort to control the fire of feelings that is burning. Fear . . . sadness . . . anxiety . . . joy . . . excitement . . . happiness . . . boredom . . . However they may appear, make no effort to douse the flames but simply let them burn.

Simply allow the fire of feelings to dance freely and wildly. Like a great forest fire, let this fire consume everything in sight, if that is its wish.

However the fire appears, simply let it be—if it's hot, let it be hot; if it's raging, let it rage. And if it is merely a quiet flicker, an ember, then let it be, just that.

Let the fire burn . . .

Now *be* the fire burning . . . no separation.

Everything Whispers This

When the heart looks,
the eyes no longer see
difference or distinction.
Beauty has disappeared
and now, there is
only beauty—
a wind howling
through the trees,
the dust that decorates
my window sill,
the temple bells ringing,
the silly little thought clouds
dancing through the vast
and empty sky—
it has all become the same,
one breath, breathing all things,
everything these eyes fall upon
whispering,
"Here I am."

Dive In

Imagine this present experience, what's arising right here and now, to be like a body of water.

Now consider for a moment that our ordinary (you could say habitual) relationship to this water is that we're a bit reluctant to get in. We're sort of just dipping a toe or two into the water, a part of us off somewhere else, perhaps imagining how much better the next moment might be.

Now let yourself dive into this water fully, soaked by whatever may be here, drenched by each experience that appears.

Everything Is Ending

Make
no effort
to sustain
this
experience.

Simply let
it vanish,
which it
is doing
effortlessly.

Make
no effort
to hold
in place
any feeling,
thought or
sensation.

Simply allow
them all to
disappear,
which they're
doing quite
naturally.

What Is

For a
moment,
don't try
to find
anything,
other than
what is.

The Impossibility of Holding On

How many thoughts did you have today? A hundred? A thousand? Maybe a million? Who knows? One thing is for certain though—they're all gone now! Every last one of them, vanished. The happy ones, the sad ones, all of them, gone . . . And the thousands or millions of feelings and sensations? They've all disappeared, as well.

Our experiences disappear of their own accord. We needn't do anything to bring this about. The release of each moment is effortless and spontaneous.

The sensation you're having right now—just try to keep it in place, try to keep it here, try to stop it from morphing into the next sensation. It can't be done. All that remains is the freshness of this, this that is appearing now and will soon vanish, too, like everything else.

Feel the wondrous freedom of this, the impossibility of ever holding on to anything.

We Can Never Step in the Same River

We often seem driven to find a kind of final answer, a definitive or conclusive understanding. We search for that perfect experience, that one insight that will enable us finally to say, *"Here it is. I've found it! I have finally arrived. This is the freedom I've been looking for, the relief I've been seeking all along. I am finally home."*

We long for this kind of finality, this kind of experiential or philosophical certainty. But we can never have it because whatever experience or moment of understanding we're able to arrive at, through whatever means, will be snapped away from us. Whatever insight we have will disappear. And whatever practices we engage in will never produce the same experience or insight we had a moment, a week, or a month ago. As the Greek philosopher Heraclitus pointed out, *we can never step in the same river twice.*

So we can relax, knowing that whatever is felt, whatever is realized, whatever is experienced will slip away. It must, for that is the nature of things, the nature of this dynamic, unpredictable, and ceaseless flow we call life.

Ever-Present Future

The future is simply not possible. Only in imagination does life ever happen there. And so it is with the past. There is no life in what was.

But, we could also say that like both past and future, the present is also not possible. Though the future will never be, it is also, in a sense, all that is ever happening, for what's here is never *really* here but continuously giving birth to the next thing, forever creating something fresh, something that has never been before.

No Boundary

Simply look, not in the realm of your ideas but in your direct experience. Can you find any lines of division, anything that actually separates one thing from another?

Can you find something that divides this from that, a boundary between inside and outside, or here and there?

Is there an actual line separating self and other, dividing you from the world?

Can you find a boundary between what appeared a moment ago and what is here now, a line separating what is from what will be?

This Ceaseless Dance

Whatever you imagine to be a fixed and solid thing (e.g., a body, a self, an emotion, a thought), look again and see that everything we might describe as being some "thing," whether seeming to be out there or in here, is in fact constantly moving, constantly changing, constantly in flux.

Feel the freedom of this, the release in seeing that nothing is ever holding still, that there is only ever this ceaseless dance . . . the fluidity of life!

You

What you call "you"
is ever changing,
the movement of life,
never fixed,
always fluid,
an ever-present
freshness.

Creation and Destruction

Everything is ending and yet we try to make it stop, engaged in this hopeless battle to sustain what has already disappeared, struggling to control what has already slipped through our fingers.

But each ending is also a beginning—life creating, then destroying, then creating itself over and over and over, the dying and the being born, one indistinguishable movement.

For a moment, make no effort to keep this here-and-now alive, to keep *what is* from disappearing. Let it die, which it is already doing anyway, whether you try to keep it alive or not!

Let everything vanish, naturally. And then let it be reborn as the next thing that appears.

Enjoy this dance of birth and death that is every moment.

Love

Consider love, not as a particular feeling or sentiment, but as the mystery that allows all feelings and sentiments to be, the space in which every experience exists.

Think of it as life, the very life that you are and that everything is—a great incomprehensible indivisibility, a mystery that welcomes all moments, without question or reason, because it is all moments.

Nothing More to Find

Consider the possibility that there are no correct experiences to have.

That no matter our experience, we can never be cast out of reality, never be thrown out of the totality that is life, because there is *only* the totality.

Separation isn't possible.

Let this sink in and stop you in your tracks.

There is nothing more to find . . .

Our Multidimensional Nature

For a moment, simply dive head first into your experience. Whether you label it as thought, feeling, sensation—or the awareness that knows each of these—matters not. Simply feel into whatever presents itself experientially. Look, and as you do, ask yourself, *"Is anything here but vast, boundless space? Can I find anything in direct experience that is not completely wide open, anything about this present perception that has either border or boundary?"* Feel into this endlessness. Is anything at the center of it? Or is the center also just endless, boundless, indivisible space? Feel into the depth, the immensity of this endless, wide-open space. How unfathomable it is . . .

As organisms, we're quite accustomed (by necessity really) to know our more bounded nature. As body-mind creatures we are, in a sense, condensed versions of this wide-open space that is life, limited and clearly defined. As this distinct and bounded organism, I am neither the tree nor the flower nor you. I am separate. I have distinction. There's a kind of boundary in experience between what is "self" and what is "other."

However, this is only part of what we are, even if it's where so much of our attention and identity tends to reside. And it's the other part that so many of the world's spiritual/contemplative traditions are focused on, helping us as organisms to discover another aspect of what we are, our space-like nature, the aspect of us that's not merely bounded, not merely closed and limited, but also wide open and without limitation.

This Fresh Moment

No matter how many
experiences of insight
or realization may
have visited us,
we remain left
with just this,
this fresh moment
that has never been before
and will never be again.

A Wind Born of Air

Like a breeze
blowing through
the empty sky,
we have never
been apart
from that which
gave us birth,
a wind born
of air.

Absolute and Relative Medicine

We could say there are two types of medicine. The first, let's call "relative medicine." It is the type we are most familiar with and encompasses the myriad strategies we employ in an effort to change our selves or our experiences in order to be restored to greater health and well-being. Sometimes, the medicines are relatively benign and quite helpful such as taking an aspirin to help ease the pain of a headache, practicing deep breathing to calm our selves down or utilizing the support of a therapist in order to feel less anxious or depressed. Other times, however, we might utilize less beneficial remedies to try to alter our body-mind states such as drinking excessively to feel less anxious or depressed.

But there is another type of medicine altogether, one that while known throughout time has remained largely hidden from view. And this other medicine, we could call the "ultimate medicine." To put it most simply, *the ultimate medicine is the realization that no remedy was ever required for us to be profoundly okay and well,* that regardless of the particular thoughts, feelings and sensations we may be experiencing in any given moment, wholeness is already present, as those very experiences.

The ultimate medicine is really the discovery that we are an inseparable part and expression of life and that as that life, we have never actually been broken. From the experiential vantage of the ultimate medicine, health/wholeness is not some state we must achieve (through hard work and practice) but rather the ever-present, natural condition of *all* body-mind states. Unlike the many relative medicines human beings utilize, the ultimate medicine isn't really a remedy one takes or a strategy one employs but is instead, what we are. We *are* the ultimate medicine in the sense that as expressions of life, we have only ever been whole and complete, as we are, with nothing needing to be done to make it so. Nature has never been split or divided; it is singular and whole. And we are an inseparable part of that same, unbroken nature and wholeness.

While the discovery of the ultimate medicine doesn't preclude the use of any relative medicine, there is now a much vaster context for all that we experience and any actions we might decide to take in response to that experience. For example, if anxiety is arising experientially, we might take a breath to calm down or if it's really strong, maybe even a drug or herb to help ourselves to relax. But as we discover that states like anxiety, rather than being signs that something within us is broken and in need of repair are in fact, a natural expression of life itself, the reflexive need for relative medicines, self-help strategies or antidotes to address (i.e., manage or control) our body-mind states will naturally relax and diminish.

All the time, energy and money spent trying to change our experiences in order to feel better, happier, or more loved will naturally lessen as a function of realizing an entirely different order of well-being, one that is not dictated, as convention would have it, by the presence or absence of particular mental, emotional or physical states.

Our capacity to feel more rather than less, to allow an ever wider and deeper range of experiences without reflexively seeing them as either sources of or obstacles to well-being brings with it a tremendous sense of freedom and empowerment, the capacity to be present with and embrace more and more of life in all its unpredictability and uncontrollability, to love what is, even as we may still, at times, be moved to transform it.

Why Even Write This Book: A Postscript

Having gotten through at least some (or maybe all of this book), you might find yourself asking the question, why?

What, for example, is the point of relaxing our efforts to arrive at some other experience or state of mind?

What is the value of recognizing that our experiences are not actually capable of being fully captured by the net of our conceptual and linguistic frameworks?

Why place attention on awareness itself? And, what's the point of recognizing that no clear dividing line can be found between awareness (what knows) and the content of awareness (what is known)?

In many ways, the answers to such questions can only come about by taking up the experiment and finding out for your self, what if any value there might be in such meditative inquiries. That being said, I can offer my own perspective on why I think it's a worthwhile endeavor to reflect upon and explore in one's direct experience, the inquiries and meditations offered in this little book.

Several years ago, I conducted a qualitative study examining how involvement with various awareness-based teachings and practices had impacted people's lives. The findings from this small study coupled with my own experiences and insights reveal several things that answer the "so what" questions I've posed above.

1. By relaxing our efforts to manipulate experience, we increasingly feel a sense of "at-home-ness" in the midst of

whatever thoughts, feelings and sensations may be occurring, even those conventionally labeled as "negative."

2. The less we seek fulfillment in some future moment, the more deeply we are able to appreciate how much is already present, how rich, how remarkable, and how miraculous each instant of life actually is.

3. As we relax the habit of trying to rearrange our thoughts, feelings and sensations in order to feel a greater sense of well-being or fulfillment, we gain familiarity with a different "order" or domain of well-being altogether, one that is not defined by the presence or absence of particular experiences but is recognized to be present in and as the very flow of experiencing itself.

4. The more we come to see that our thoughts are simply *interpretations* of rather than absolutely true statements about the nature of reality, the less locked into, identified with or beholden to our own points of view we will be. This in turn leads to more open-mindedness, a relaxing of the habitual tendency to reflexively defend our ideas or ideologies, and greater cognitive and emotional flexibility.

5. The more we recognize that experiences can never be adequately captured by any of our conceptual, philosophical, or linguistic frameworks, the more we discover something about ourselves (and life) that lies utterly beyond any and all descriptions and interpretations, an unfathomable, mysterious, and ineffable depth.

6. That which is aware of this moment is naturally open to it; what is aware of experiences is effortlessly accepting those experiences; and that which is aware of the arising and passing away of phenomena is not struggling

with those phenomena. And so, as we bring attention to awareness itself, these naturally occurring qualities (i.e., openness, acceptance, non-struggle) tend to come more and more alive in our direct experience.

7. As we recognize that no clear lines of division can be found experientially between awareness and its phenomenal content, we become more aware of another dimension of our humanness, namely an aspect of us that is unbounded, without division or separation, and freed from the tyranny of self-focus and its energy draining project of propping up, defending and protecting itself from whatever it imagines might threaten its psychological integrity and security. The recognition that what we call "self" is not as substantial, fixed or bounded as we imagined frees up tremendous energy as the habitual grasping and striving to obtain satisfaction for that imagined self, relaxes.

Made in United States
Troutdale, OR
09/29/2024

23235430R00060